PORTRAIT OF
PLYMOUTH

Lee Pengelly

HALSGROVE

First published in Great Britain in 2009

Copyright © Lee Pengelly 2009

Title page: *Seagull, Barbican*

British Library Cataloguing-in-Publication Data
A CIP record for this title is available from the British Library

ISBN 978 1 84114 816 8

HALSGROVE
Halsgrove House,
Ryelands Industrial Estate,
Bagley Road, Wellington, Somerset TA21 9PZ
Tel: 01823 653777   Fax: 01823 216796
email: sales@halsgrove.com

Part of the Halsgrove group of companies
Information on all Halsgrove titles is available at: www.halsgrove.com

Printed and bound by Grafiche Flaminia, Italy

For Abi & Zak - the lights of my life.

INTRODUCTION

As a Plymouthian I was delighted to be asked to produce a book of images on my home town. I have lived and worked in Plymouth for all of my 37 years although it has only been within the last ten years that I have grown to appreciate my surroundings through my photography.

The city is constantly changing with new views opening up, new buildings emerging on the skyline and whole areas of redevelopment underway. The most recent major development being the new Drake's Circus shopping precinct which has completely changed the city. I have tried to include the familiar places such as the seafront and city centre but also some hidden gems on the outskirts of the city too. A mix of buildings, landscapes, people and nature all combining to build a picture of Plymouth today.

As a photographer I am spoilt for choice for subjects and locations to shoot. Apart from the city I have Dartmoor on my doorstep, the beautiful South Devon coastline and parts of the Tamar Valley all within a half hour of home.

It is easy to take your surroundings for granted and miss what your home turf has to offer. I still feel like I am only scratching the surface but I hope to be able to carry on capturing the city as it evolves over many years to come.

In parallel with the city my photographic style is constantly evolving too; this book showcases my new up-to-date work alongside my older work. One thing is constant through my photography and that is the quality of light. I like to produce most of my work during the hours of dawn and dusk and this book is no exception.

The challenge of city photography is knowing what not to include in the frame; many views in the book have been shot after careful planning and often re-visiting so as not to include scaffolding, white vans and the like.

Over the past ten years I have produced many images of the Plymouth area both on film and digital mediums. This book contains a selection of images on various formats, from 5x4" large format and medium format transparency film to my current digital set up. I am now dedicated to the digital medium and have used the Nikon D2x for the majority of the book. A selection of lenses from 10mm to 300mm have been used to capture the images along with neutral density graduate and polariser filters.

Lee Pengelly
www.silverscenephoto.co.uk

Acknowledgements

I would like to thank the following for help in producing this book.

Jan Barwick - *Devon Life*
Jessop's - Plymouth
Spectrum Photo Labs - Plymouth
Tourist Information - Plymouth
Plymouth City Council
Rick Cowdery at Home Park
My Wife - for her patience when the light's good

Plymouth Sound. A dusky sky over the Sound. Moored boats in the distance await the start of the annual firework competition which are let off from Mountbatten pier.

The Tamar bridges span the River Tamar between Plymouth and Saltash. When Isambard Kingdom Brunel designed and built the Royal Albert bridge he envisaged a gateway to Cornwall. To this day both the rail and road bridge are constantly busy. Recent widening of the road bridge has eased traffic chaos, especially during the summer months.

Tamar dawn. A disused boat on the banks of the River Tamar at Saltash Passage.

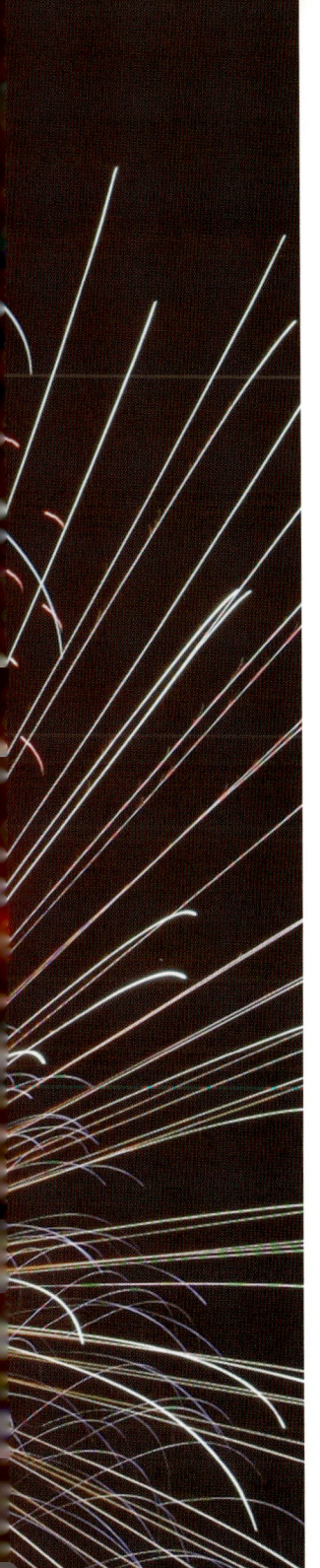

Left: National Firework Championships, Plymouth Hoe. Each year in August Plymouth is very fortunate to host the Championships where firework companies compete with brilliant displays.

Top: Christmas rides, City Centre. Plymouth's town centre at Christmas, where traditional fairground rides, markets and other festivities give the city centre a festive feel each year.

Above: Cars driving on and off the Torpoint ferry at dusk.

Bickham sunset. Late spring on the edge of Dartmoor near Roborough.

Hoe diving board. Despite its rusting dilapidated state the diving board below Plymouth Hoe is transformed by the early dawn light on a winter morning. This could even be the edge of Lake Garda!

Above: Plymouth Hoe at dawn.
Left: Smeaton's Tower stands sentinel over Plymouth Hoe.

Above: Interior stonework of the ruined Charles Cross church.
Right: A view of Plympton at dawn from the castle. The original castle was constructed by the First Earl of Devon, Richard de Redvers, in the reign of King Henry I. It is built on the site of a Roman fort.

Elizabethan House, Barbican. This late 1500s sea captains house was rescued from demolition in 1929. The narrow cobbled streets protect its frontage from the worst of the weather.

Sutton Harbour, Barbican. A picture postcard view of the historic Barbican where colourful fishing boats remind us of Plymouth's once great fishing industry.

Buckland Abbey. This 700 year old building was the former home of Sir Francis Drake. Now owned by the National Trust, among its many other treasures it houses Drake's Drum.

National Marine Aquarium. Opened in 1998 the Aquarium houses a 'Moorland Stream to Ocean Water' feature, complete with a variety of species. In 2002 the aquarium was extended and now boasts a huge shark theatre.

The Charles Cross roundabout has witnessed many changes over the years, and now in its modern guise it forms a spectacular gateway to the city.

Left: A lone dog walker takes a stroll along a beech-lined avenue in Autumn at Central Park.
Above: Spectacular pink blossom on trees beside the bowling green on Plymouth Hoe.

Left: Smeaton's Tower, Plymouth Hoe, viewed from below the fire beacon.

Above: The Stars and Stripes flapping in the wind above the Mayflower Steps.

Francis Drake's statue, Plymouth Hoe. Drake famously refused to leave Plymouth to confront the Spanish Armada in 1588 until he had finished his game of bowls on the Hoe.

The diving board near Plymouth's art deco seafront has stood the test of time. Battered by storms and salt water it has seen better days but hopefully this iconic Plymouth landmark will one day be restored to its former glory.

Tinside Lido. Originally opened in 1913 the public swimming bath has changed over the years. In the thirties new art deco terraces and a bathing house were added. It fell into disrepair in the eighties but was transformed and re-opened in 2003.

Small fishing boats on Hooe
Lake.

A lone yacht at sunset at Millbrook estuary.

Left: Plympton St Maurice. The oldest part of the town was once a busy trading port, famous for tin. It is the birthplace of the artist Sir Joshua Reynolds.

Above: Plympton Guildhall. The present building stands on the site of the original thirteenth-century hall in this narrow street.

Above: Plympton St Maurice Church. The parish church of St Maurice viewed through the arches of the old Grammar School.

Right: Sheepstor view. The small village of
Sheepstor on the edge of Dartmoor, north-east of
Plymouth.
Above: Plym Weir, Plymbridge, showing the
autumn woodland colours.

Waves rushing out over Wembury beach at dusk.

Storm clouds move in from the west over Mountbatten Pier, dwarfing Plymouth Hoe.

Left: The early dawn light catches the autumnal colours in Pounds Park.
Above: Pounds House stands in Pounds Park which is part of Central Park in the city.

Left: Sutton Harbour. At dawn this normally busy stretch of cafés, bars and restaurants is a tranquil haven for photography.

Right: The Three Crowns, on the Barbican, one of Plymouth's popular harbourside pubs.

Columns detail of the Belvedere on Plymouth Hoe.

Dawn light on the Belvedere, or 'Wedding Cake', as it's known locally.

Duke of Cornwall Hotel. This grand Grade II listed Victorian hotel is a prominent landmark for locals and visitors alike.

The tower was purely decorative, although porters at the hotel once used it as a lookout to watch for approaching ocean liners coming into Plymouth.

Summer dawn over Sutton Harbour on Plymouth's old Barbican.

Left: Barbican waterfront. A small water taxi runs from here taking passengers to and from Mountbatten, a popular service especially during the summer months.
Above: The river Plym at Shaugh Prior during the autumn.

Skeletal remains of an old timber boat overlooking the still waters at Hooe Lake, Plymstock.

Late winter sun bursts through cloud over Plymouth Sound at Bovisand bay.

The unmistakable sight of a Brittany Ferry leaving Plymouth for the coast of France. While in dock the *Pont Aven* dwarfs the surrounding buildings, but once in the Sound it soon disappears from view on its cross Channel journey.

Mountbatten. A fishing trawler returning to port.

Warm morning sunshine on the River Yealm at Newton Ferrers.

At the start of the day,
early morning sunrise is
reflected in the River Yealm
at Newton Ferrers.

Smeaton's Tower, Plymouth Hoe. This unmistakable red and white 72-feet-high lighthouse on Plymouth Hoe has become synonymous with the city. Originally built on the Eddystone reef in 1759 it was later taken down and moved block-by-block in the early 1800s to its present position on the Hoe.

Smeaton's Tower
silhouetted against
a vivid sunset.

Fairground, Plymouth Hoe.

This big wheel was erected beside the Civic Centre during the Christmas period, dubbed the 'Plymouth Eye' by some!

The Plymouth Pavilions. Built on the former Millbay Railway Station site, Plymouth's very own 4000-seater stadium has played host to many big name bands and artists over the years.

Home Park. No book on Plymouth would be complete without a reference to Plymouth Argyle Football Club. Originally built in 1893, Home Park held its first professional football match in 1903. In the 1990s the grounds and stadium were improved to their current 20 000 seater design. Come on you Greens!

Drake's Circus. When the site was cleared to make way for the new development tons of concrete were removed. Over 95 per cent of materials removed were then recycled.

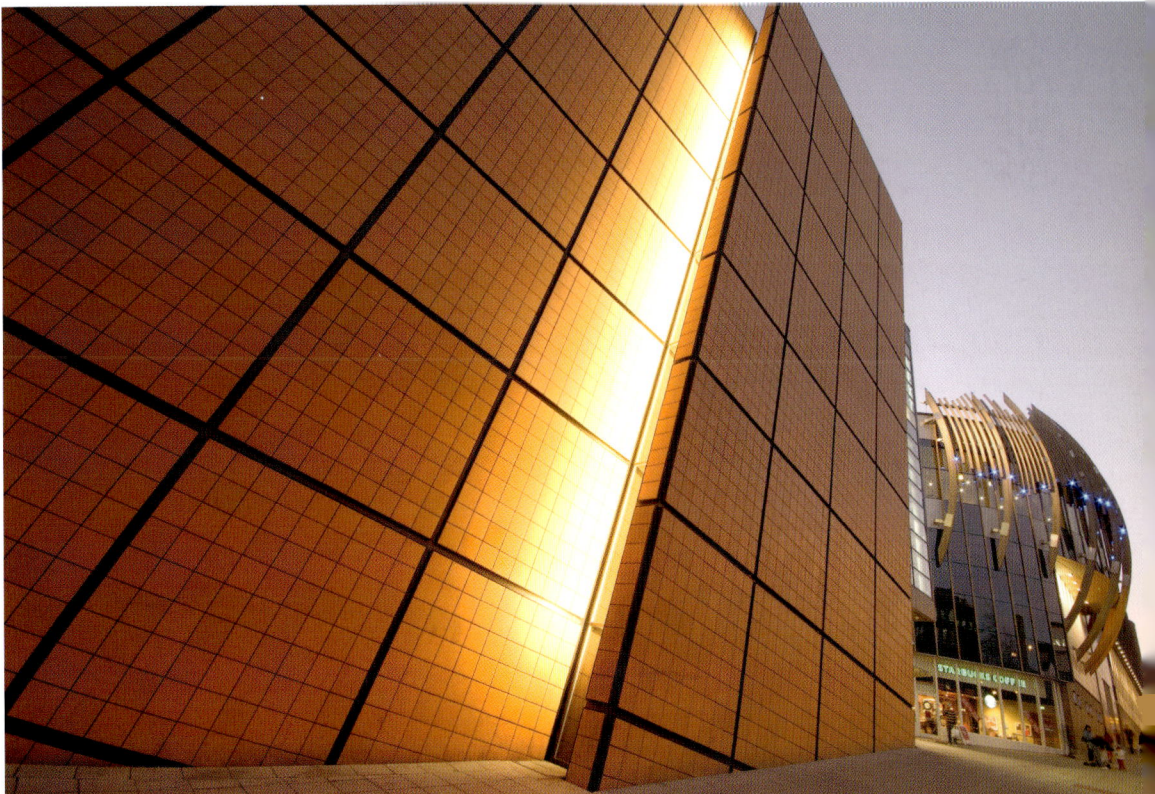

Old Mill Café, Wembury. This former mill house, overlooking Wembury beach, is now a popular café and gift shop owned by the National Trust.

Fort Stamford, Hooe. This five-sided defensive fort is now a Scheduled Ancient Monument.

A fiery sunset over Meavy on the edge of Dartmoor. The moor provides a superb recreational area for those who live in nearby Plymouth.

Head high oilseed rape surround this old barn above the Plym valley.

Top: Peek Hill, Dartmoor. This stunted hawthorn tree marks one of the gateway's onto the moors, the view from here stretches down over to Plymouth Sound.
Above: Autumn in Plymbridge woods.

Merchants House, Barbican. One of the largest and finest examples of late sixteenth-century housing. During the seventeenth century this building was home to three Plymouth mayors.

Right: The Royal Citadel. Built in 1665 this huge fort was the most important English defence for over 100 years. It is still used as a military base and boasts a prominent position overlooking Plymouth Sound.

Barbican Glassworks. This former Victorian fish market now houses a glass and steel visitor centre. Luckily the original architecture has been preserved; old and new at its best.

Home of the *Western Morning News* and Plymouth's own newspaper the *Evening Herald*, this impressive glass and steel structure at Derriford was designed in the form of a huge ship.

Flete House, Ermington. This Victorian mansion was built between 1878 and 1885 for Henry Bingham Mildmay of Barings Bank. Now converted into apartments, it overlooks the River Erme.

Crownhill Fort. The largest of a ring of eleven forts and batteries which were completed in 1872. They were built to form the northern part of Plymouth's defences. This fort is the only one in it's original condition.

Left: The memorial on Plymouth Hoe to the men of the Devonshire, Somerset and Gloucestershire Regiments who laid down their lives in the South African War.

Above: This Plymouth war memorial is dedicated to all those who lost their lives in the Great War from 1914–1918. Reading the names on the plaques surrounding the memorial is very sobering.

Left: St Peter's Church, Wyndham Square. This recently refurbished church is visible from various parts of the city, including my office window! Its ornate stonework catches the early evening light from the west.

Above: Spring blossom behind St Andrew's Church in Buckwell Street.

Right: The copper spire of Catherine Street Baptist Chapel was added in 1959, the original chapel was another victim of the Blitz bombs.

Colourful beach changing huts below the Hoe.

The Corinthian Yacht Club has a prominent position overlooking Plymouth Sound.

Above: *Jessie Lou*, Barbican. The rusty nameplate of a fishing trawler moored in Sutton Harbour.
Left: Sutton Harbour on the Barbican is a busy port for Plymouth's fishermen, although the industry is struggling.

This unusual sculpture on the Barbican, dubbed by locals 'The Prawn', is a strange mix of various sea creatures.

The £200 million redevelopment of the old Drake's Circus site was a welcome development although once built the new shopping precinct design has caused some controversy. Love it or hate it, it definitely makes a statement.

Sainsbury's supermarket - This unusual building is often overlooked but its functional quirky design is the first thing to greet visitors to the city approaching from the A38 Expressway.

Park benches at dawn on Plymouth Hoe.

An early morning stroll through Plymouth's Central Park on a crisp autumn morning. The Park is Trust Land and therefore cannot be built on, providing a haven for joggers, dog walkers and families all year round.

Previous page: Dawn light over Sutton Marina and Plymouth city centre
Above: A vibrant crop of oilseed rape on the edge of Wembury village.

Plympton St Mary's Church. This beautiful church dates from 1311 when it was part of the old priory. Some of my relatives are buried in this quiet churchyard.

Left: Victoria Cottages.   Quaint dwellings on Church Street below Plympton castle.
Above: The Barbican Theatre, a centre for the performing arts.

Ornamental gardens surround the Valentis Café on Plymouth Hoe.

Guildhall window. During the Christmas period Plymouth's Guildhall is illuminated with blue lighting picking out lovely detailing such as these window arches.

The ruin of Charles Cross Church remains as a reminder of the Blitz. This prominent landmark stands at the new gateway to the city with Drake's Circus development positioned behind.

The stone arch of Mayflower Steps frames a view of Mountbatten in the distance. The Pilgrim Fathers left Plymouth from this point in September 1620 destined for America aboard the *Mayflower* with 102 passengers.

The Distillery, Barbican. Home of Plymouth Gin which has been made from a secret recipe since 1793. One of Plymouth's oldest buildings, it dates back to 1431. It is rumoured the Pilgrim Fathers spent their last night here before embarking for America.

Above: Winter sunset over Bovisand Bay near Plymouth.
Left: Evening light catches the magnificent architecture of Royal William Yard. This former dockyard building now incorporates luxury apartments.

Left: Early Edwardian Baroque styling decorates the facade of the City of Plymouth Museum and Art Gallery. Gutted in the 1941 Blitz it was restored in 1954 and now holds fine art, natural and human history exhibits.

Right: The Roland Levinsky Building, named after the former Vice-Chairman of Plymouth University. This striking copper-clad building was built in 2007. It is home to the Arts and Architecture faculties of the University.

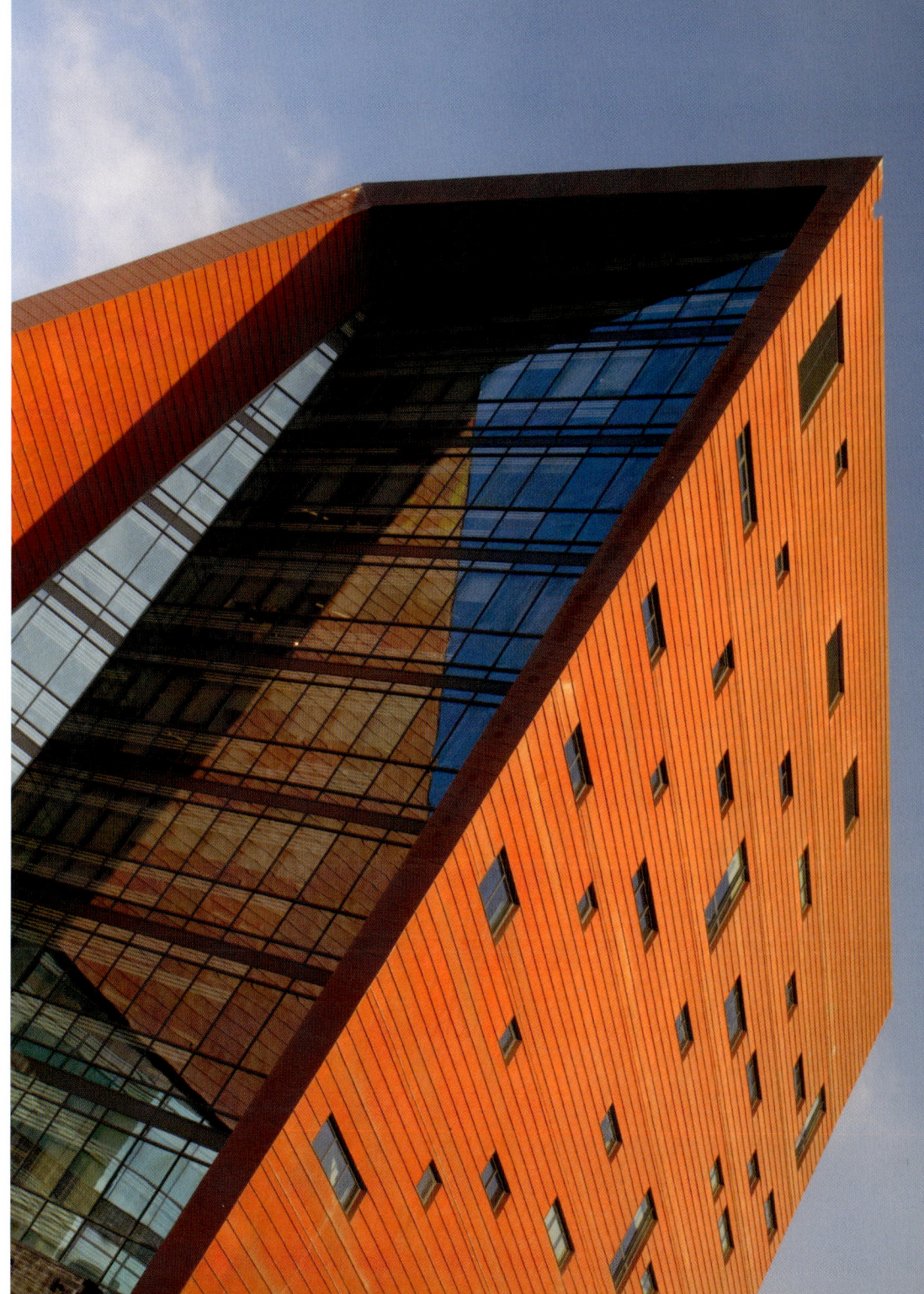

Previous page: Drake's Island viewed from the jetty at Firestone Bay.
Left: The Book Cupboard shop at Mitre Court on the Barbican.

Traditional fudge shop on the Barbican.

Autumn at the National Trust's Saltram House.

The Crescent, Mountbatten. This modern crescent-shaped block of luxury apartments occupies an enviable position overlooking Mountbatten bay.

Right: Dawn, and a mute swan glides on Hooe lake in Plymstock.
Far right: A lone yacht catches first light on Hooe Lake.

Left: Archway detail of the former Plympton Grammar School. The Jacobean Gothic style school was built in 1664, Sir Joshua Reynolds' father was a master here.

Right: Saltram House. This National Trust Georgian mansion stands in 500 acres of beautiful grounds. It was used as a location for the film 'Sense and Sensibility'.

Right: St Andrew's Church stands on Royal Parade in the city centre.

Far right: The ruins of Charles Cross Church rise alongside the new shopping centre.

Drake's Island, viewed from the conical copper rooftop of the Dome on a summer morning.

The new Armada Way Piazza is now lined with silver birch trees and minimalist chrome benches, striking in its simplicity.

The small beach at Wembury becomes deserted during winter months leaving the elements to do their work.

Grey Heron, Plymbridge.
Plym woods is a great place
to spot wildlife. Herons,
kingfishers, even otters can be
seen here if you are lucky.

A Brittany ferry dwarfs Mountbatten pier on its return to Plymouth.

Barbican dawn.

Left: The Dome, Plymouth Hoe. This award winning visitor centre has sadly been closed to the public for the past few years. There are plans to change its use and to re-open this unusual building.

Right: The Guildhall and County and Crown court in Plymouth city centre.

Left: Artillery Tower, Firestone Bay. The Artillery Tower dates from the early 1500s and is one of the oldest complete military towers on Plymouth's seafront. It is now a popular restaurant.
Below: Mountbatten Tower. This Scheduled Ancient Monument was built in 1652 as a gun tower protecting the entrance to Plymouth's harbour.

The clock tower
of the former
technical college.

Plymouth's Money Centre building remained functional during the rebuilding of the Drake's Circus shopping complex, but the area around it is now completely changed

The Diver statue outside Drake's Circus shopping precinct.

Architectural detail of Drake's Circus shopping precinct.

The Admiral McBride pub on Plymouth's Barbican.

The Roundabout Pub. This little round pub is now dwarfed by the new Roland Levinsky building. It is popular with the student population of Plymouth.

Far left: The grounds of Saltram House come alive during early spring with the arrival of new growth. The plants and grasses around this old oak provide welcome nourishment for Saltram's resident cattle.

Left: An oak tree sapling takes shape amongst the hoar frost in the arboretum at Burrator on the edge of Dartmoor.

Dawn over Plymouth Sound from Mountbatten pier.

The Gothic tower of Plymouth's Guildhall.

The Guildhall survived the first night of the Blitz in 1941 but was unfortunately gutted by fire during the nights of 20 and 21 March that year. It was rebuilt in 1953 and re-opened in 1959.

This 27 feet high stainless steel sundial was designed by Carole Vincent from Boscastle in Cornwall. Apparently it runs 1 hour and 17 minutes behind local clocks.

Lenkiewicz mural. One of Plymouth's renowned artists, born in 1941 Robert Lenkiewicz was certainly a memorable character. This mural was painted by him in 1971 and remains to this day as a reminder of his work. The painting has been temporarily battened to protect its fragility.

Plymouth Hoe jetty - dawn
over Plymouth Sound.

Above: Young Mallard ducklings contemplate a swim on the edge of Radford lake in Plymstock.

Left: Burrator reservoir, Dartmoor. One of Plymouth's water sources this huge area of water is managed by the South West Lakes Trust. It is a beautiful spot popular with locals and tourists.

Union Street. The 'Street' was originally built to link Devonport and Plymouth and was laid out between 1812 and 1820. Designed by John Foulston the grand boulevard bears little resemblance to its former glory now.

Theatre Royal. Plymouth's main theatre on Royal Parade has hosted a variety of first class musicals and shows over the years.

Above: The Royal Bank of Scotland building at the top of Royal Parade. Left: The Bank. Originally opened as a bank in 1888 by Wilts and Dorset Banking Company this magnificent building is now a popular bar and restaurant.

Above: Albert Road Clock. There are two towers at the Albert road end of the Dockyard, one contains this clock and the other a 'hooter', a siren which sounds to remind Dockyardies that it's break time!

Left: Drake's Clock. The four-faced clock tower at the entrance to Drake Naval base runs on weights which run the full height of the tower and underground.

Right: Derry's Clock. No book on Plymouth would be complete without a picture of Derry's Clock. This little clock holds a special place in the hearts of many Plymouthians. It survived the Blitz and remains in its original position. Officially it is a fountain but ironically has never been linked to a water supply.

Fort Bovisand. Evening sunset lights up the old Fort overlooking Bovisand beach. One of 22 forts built in Plymouth to guard against attack from the French in the nineteenth century. The fort is now a renowned dive school.

Golden Hind. This replica of Francis Drake's famous galleon is all that remains of the former Drake Cinema at Derry's Cross.